LIGHTNING BOLT BOOKS™

Angel Sharks in Action

Buffy Silverman

Lerner Publications ◆ Minneapolis

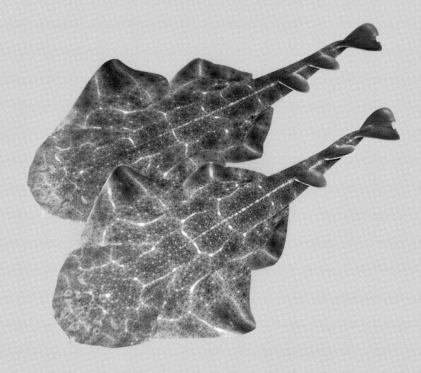

Lerner Publications Company
A division of Lerner Publishing Group, Inc.
241 First Avenue North
Minneapolis, MN 55401 USA

For reading levels and more information, look up this title at www.lernerbooks.com.

Library of Congress Cataloging-in-Publication Data

Names: Silverman, Buffy, author.
Title: Angel sharks in action / Buffy Silverman.
Description: Minneapolis : Lerner Publications, [2017] | Series: Lightning bolt books. Shark world |
    Audience: Ages 6-9. | Audience: K to grade 3. | Includes bibliographical references and index.
Identifiers: LCCN 2016042313 (print) | LCCN 2016045062 (ebook) | ISBN 9781512433814
    (lb : alk. paper) | ISBN 9781512455939 (pb : alk. paper) | ISBN 9781512450606 (eb pdf)
Subjects: LCSH: Squatinidae—Juvenile literature. | Sharks—Juvenile literature.
Classification: LCC QL638.95.S88 S55 2017 (print) | LCC QL638.95.S88 (ebook) | DDC 597.3—dc23

LC record available at https://lccn.loc.gov/2016042313

Manufactured in the United States of America
1-42017-23887-12/2/2016

Table of Contents

Meet an Angel Shark

A Pacific angel shark lies buried in the sand. The eyes on top of its head peek out. It waits without moving. Other fish do not notice the angel shark.

The flat-bodied shark bursts out to chase a fish. It opens its mouth wide. *Snap!* The shark grabs its prey.

Angel sharks hunt in the Atlantic Ocean, the Pacific Ocean, and the Indian Ocean.

The Pacific angel shark is one kind of angel shark. There are eighteen other kinds too. They live in sandy sea bottoms and near coral reefs. They swim near bays.

Pacific angel sharks are one of the most studied kinds of angel sharks.

Pacific angel sharks move around at night. They spend their days buried in sand. Angel sharks can be black, brown, red, or gray. Their colors blend with the rocky bottom.

Angels Grow Up

Sharks are fish. Many fish lay their eggs in water. But angel shark eggs grow inside their mom. The babies are called pups.

After ten months, the eggs hatch. The mother gives birth to six to ten pups.

Great white sharks are one animal that may eat angel sharks.

The pups are born in the spring. They swish their tail fins and swim away from mom. They are ready to live on their own. But many pups will not survive. Bigger animals eat them.

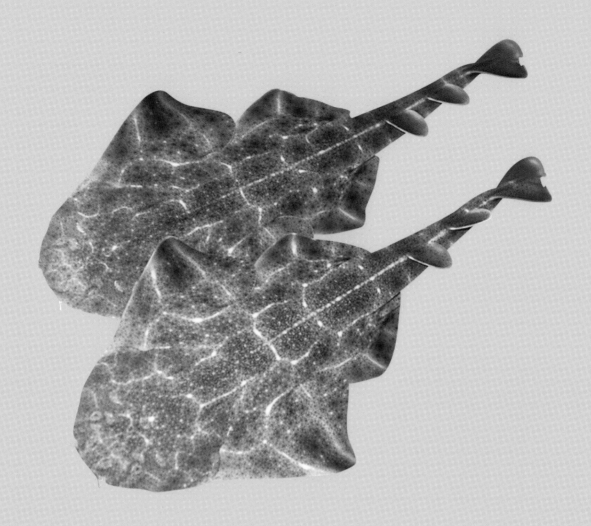

Angel shark pups grow slowly. Male angel sharks become adults in eight years. Females grow until they are thirteen years old. Then they are ready to have pups of their own.

Most angel sharks stop growing when they are about 5 feet (1.5 meters) long. That's about the size of a twelve-year-old child. Angel sharks can live for thirty-five years.

An adult angel shark weighs about 60 pounds (27 kilograms).

Hidden Below

An angel shark can sense prey while it hides in the sand. Its eyes watch for movement.

The sharks have special organs near their mouths called barbels. They use barbels to taste and feel.

Do you see the angel shark's barbels?

An angel shark's mouth
is at the tip of its snout.
Rows and rows of sharp,
pointy teeth spear its prey.

Sharks often lose their
teeth when they bite prey.
Sharks grow thousands of
new teeth during their lives.

Like all fish, angel sharks breathe oxygen from water using gills. The shark pumps water through the mouth. It also pumps water through openings on the head called spiracles. The water goes over the gills and out through gill slits.

Pacific angel sharks have five pairs of gill slits.

Angel on a Hunt

An angel shark can lie motionless for days at a time. Its flat body and winglike fins blend into the bottom. It waits and waits for prey.

Can you see the angel shark hidden in the sand?

A large fish swims nearby. The hidden angel shark comes to life. It snaps up its head. Its throat swells, and it sucks in its prey.

The shark's jaws snap shut and trap its meal. In less than a second, the prey disappears inside the shark.

Angel sharks hunt fish, squid, octopuses, and clams.

Soon other animals learn that an angel shark hides below. They stay away. Then the shark swims to another area. It burrows in the sand and waits for another meal to come by.

Diagram

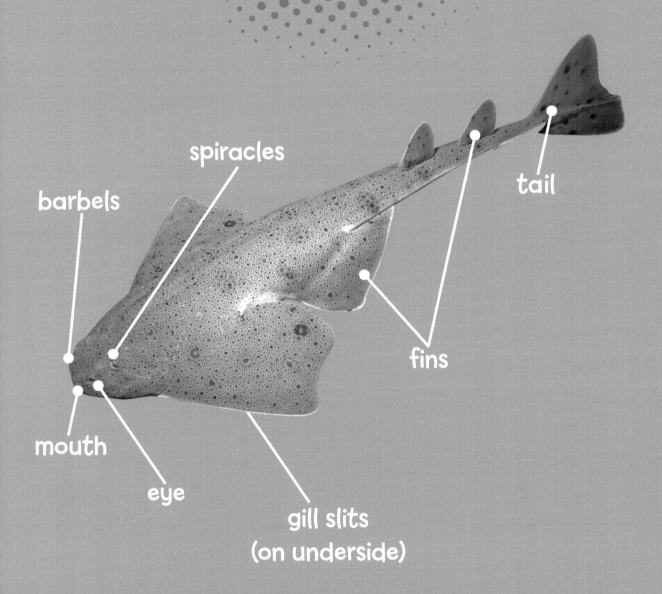

spiracles

barbels

tail

fins

mouth

eye

gill slits
(on underside)

Angel Sharks and People

- You won't see an angel shark if you're swimming at the beach. But divers sometimes find angel sharks. An angel shark only bites a diver if the diver bothers the shark.

- People began catching Pacific angel sharks for food about thirty-five years ago. They trapped them with nets.

- Angel sharks were in danger of dying out because of fishing. Laws were passed to limit the number of angel sharks that fishing boat crews can catch.

Glossary

barbel: a whisker-like organ growing near the mouth of an angel shark

coral reef: a hard ridge in the ocean where many animals and plants live

gill slit: an opening on the side of an angel shark through which water passes

oxygen: gas in air and water that plants and animals need to survive

prey: an animal that is hunted for food

snout: the nose and mouth of an animal

spiracle: a breathing hole on a shark's head

Further Reading

All about Sharks—Pacific Angel Shark
http://www.enchantedlearning.com/subjects/sharks/species/Angelshark.shtml

Discovery Channel. *Sharkopedia: The Complete Guide to Everything Shark.* Des Moines: Time, 2013.

Discovery Kids: Sharks
http://discoverykids.com/category/sharks/

FantasticAnimal: Angel Shark vs. Horned Shark
https://www.youtube.com/watch?v=wtMOWiU8Cks

Gerstein, Sherry. *See-Thru Sharks.* Minneapolis: Millbrook Press, 2015.

Hansen, Grace. *Angel Sharks.* Minneapolis: Abdo Kids, 2016.

Index

Photo Acknowledgments

The images in this book are used with the permission of: CB2/ZOB/WENN.com/Newscom, pp. 2, 8, 10; © Andy Murch/Visuals Unlimited, Inc., p. 4; © Kelvin Aitken/VWPics/Alamy, pp. 5, 17, 18; © Douglas Klug/Moment Open/Getty Images, p. 6; © Gerard Soury/Oxford Scientific/Getty Images, p. 7; © MASA USHIODA/Stephen Frink Collection/Alamy, p. 9; © Phillip Colla/SeaPics.com, pp. 11, 19; © GREGORY OCHOCKI/Science Source/Getty Images, p. 12; © Mark Conlin/Alamy, pp. 13, 16; © our wonderful world/Moment/Getty Images, p. 14; © RosalreneBetancourt 10/Alamy, p. 15; © Biosphoto/SuperStock, p. 20; © Dan Burton/Minden Pictures, p. 22.

Front cover: © Gerard Soury/Oxford Scientific/Getty Images.

Main body text set in Billy Infant regular 28/36. Typeface provided by SparkType.